LOOKING AT COUNTRIES

Looking at
IRELAND

Reading consultant: Susan Nations, M.Ed.,
author/literacy coach/consultant in literacy development

Gareth Stevens
Publishing

Please visit our Web site at www.garethstevens.com.
For a free color catalog describing Gareth Stevens Publishing's list
of high-quality books, call 1-800-542-2595 (USA)
or 1-800-387-3178 (Canada). Gareth Stevens Publishing's fax: 1-877-542-2596

Library of Congress Cataloging-in-Publication Data

Pohl, Kathleen.
    Looking at Ireland / Kathleen Pohl.
       p. cm.
    Includes index.
    ISBN-10: 0-8368-8769-7   ISBN-13: 978-0-8368-8769-3 (lib. bdg.)
    ISBN-10: 0-8368-8776-X   ISBN-13: 978-0-8368-8776-1 (softcover)
    1. Ireland—Juvenile literature. I. Title.
    DA906.P64   2008
    941.7—dc22   2007027939

This edition first published in 2008 by
Gareth Stevens Publishing
A Weekly Reader® Company
1 Reader's Digest Road
Pleasantville, NY 10570-7000 USA

Copyright © 2008 by Gareth Stevens, Inc.

Senior Managing Editor: Lisa M. Guidone
Senior Editor: Barbara Bakowski
Creative Director: Lisa Donovan
Designer: Tammy West
Photo Researcher: Sylvia Ohlrich

Photo credits: (t=top, b=bottom)
Cover Will & Deni McIntyre/Corbis; title page Peter Adams Photography/Alamy; p. 4 Derek Croucher/
Alamy; p. 6 Nagelestock.com/Alamy; p. 7t Michael Diggin/Alamy; p. 7b scenicireland.com/Christopher
Hill Photographic/Alamy; p. 8 Peter Titmuss/Alamy; p. 9t Nagelestock.com/Alamy; p. 9b Daniel Barillot/
Masterfile; p. 10 Isifa Image Service s.r.o./Alamy; p. 11t Marmaduke St. John/Alamy; p. 11b Christian Kober/
Alamy; p. 12t Bill Bachmann/Alamy; p. 12b Dennis Cox/Alamy; p. 13t WireImageStock/Masterfile; p. 13b
Authors Image/Alamy; p. 14t Will & Deni McIntyre/Corbis; p. 14b AA World Travel Library/Alamy; p. 15t
David Lyons/Alamy; p. 15b Ingolf Pompe/Aurora Photos; p. 16 Art Kowalsky/Alamy; p. 17t SC Photos/Alamy;
p. 17b Liam White/Alamy; p. 18 Searagen/Alamy; p. 19t Peter Adams Photography/Alamy; p. 19b Ros Drinkwater/
Alamy; p. 20t Paul Lindsay/Alamy; p. 20b Foodfolio/Alamy; p. 21 Ralph A. Clevenger/Corbis; p. 22t Liam White/
Alamy; p. 22b Gideon Mendel/Corbis; p. 23t Bill Bachmann/Alamy; p. 23b Marshall Ikonography/Alamy; p. 24
Julian Herbert/Getty Images; p. 25t scenicireland.com/Christopher Hill Photographic/Alamy; p. 25b Michael Diggin/
Alamy; p. 26 Paul Thompson Images/Alamy; p. 27t Richard Naude/Alamy; p. 27b Javier Larrea/SuperStock

Printed in the United States of America

1 2 3 4 5 6 7 8 9 10 09 08 07

Contents

Words that appear in the glossary are printed in **boldface** type the first time they occur in the text.

Where Is Ireland?

Ireland is a small country in northwestern Europe. It takes up most of an island in the Atlantic Ocean. A small area of the island, in the northeast, is called Northern Ireland. Northern Ireland is part of a different country, the United Kingdom.

Did you know?

All of Ireland was once ruled by Great Britain. That country is now the United Kingdom.

The Custom House in Ireland's capital, Dublin, houses government offices.

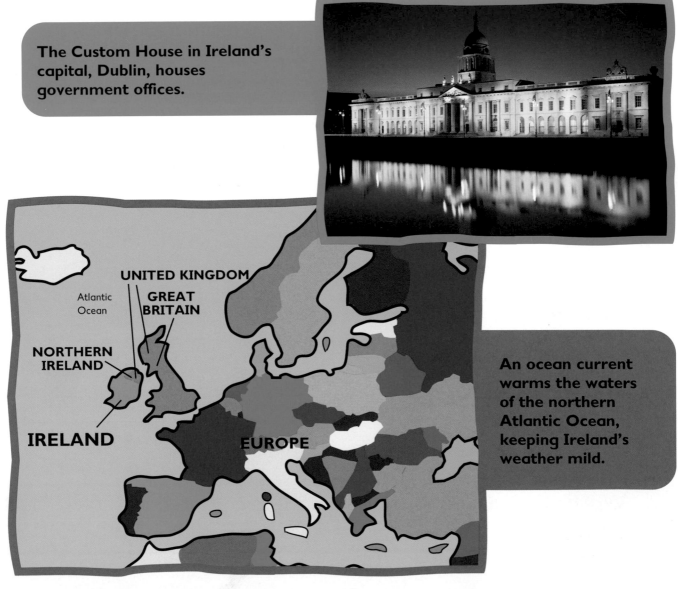

UNITED KINGDOM

Atlantic Ocean

GREAT BRITAIN

NORTHERN IRELAND

IRELAND

EUROPE

An ocean current warms the waters of the northern Atlantic Ocean, keeping Ireland's weather mild.

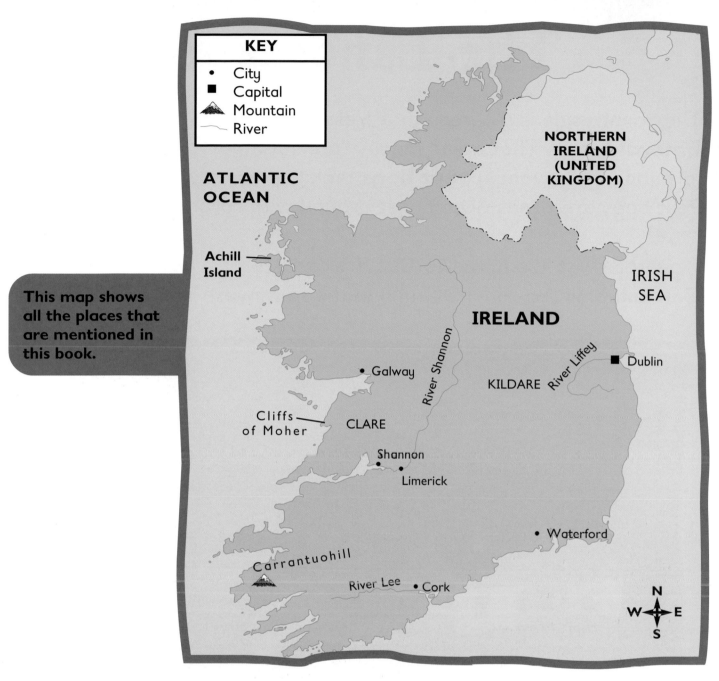

KEY
- • City
- ■ Capital
- 🏔 Mountain
- ～ River

ATLANTIC OCEAN

NORTHERN IRELAND (UNITED KINGDOM)

Achill Island

IRISH SEA

IRELAND

This map shows all the places that are mentioned in this book.

River Shannon

River Liffey

KILDARE

■ Dublin

• Galway

Cliffs of Moher

CLARE

Shannon •

• Limerick

• Waterford

Carrantuohill

River Lee • Cork

N
W E
S

On the east, the Irish Sea separates Ireland from the island of Great Britain. The Atlantic Ocean borders Ireland to the south, west, and northwest.

Ireland is an independent **republic**. It is divided into twenty-six **counties**. The capital, and largest city, is Dublin. Government and business offices, colleges, and theaters line its streets.

The Landscape

The countryside is so green that Ireland is often called the **Emerald Isle**. That name means "green island." Rolling farmland and swampy **peat bogs** make up much of Ireland. Peat bogs are areas of soft, wet ground with rotting plants.

Mountains rise along the coasts. Ireland's highest peak is Carrantuohill (ka-run-TOO-uhl) in the southwest.

Achill Island lies off the west coast of Ireland. Achill has high sea cliffs and sandy beaches. It also has farms and small villages.

The steep Cliffs of Moher are in County Clare in western Ireland.

Did you know?

Ireland has more than twelve thousand lakes. They are fed by the country's high rainfall each year.

Ireland has many sandy beaches and small islands. It also has thousands of lakes. Its longest river, the River Shannon, runs through the middle of the country.

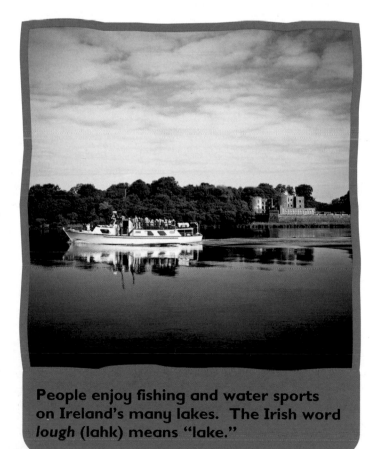

People enjoy fishing and water sports on Ireland's many lakes. The Irish word *lough* (lahk) means "lake."

Weather and Seasons

The Irish people often say their country has forty shades of green. Ireland is so green because rain falls almost every day. Ocean breezes that blow across Ireland keep the weather mild and wet.

In the low-lying areas of Ireland, about 35 inches (900 millimeters) of rain fall a year. Higher areas get up to 100 inches (2,500 mm) each year.

The sunniest and driest months are April, May, and June. In those months, most parts of Ireland get about six hours of sunshine each day. December is the dullest month, with only about one hour of sunshine daily.

Some rain falls most days in Ireland.

Irish folk tales tell of a pot of gold at the end of every rainbow.

Plenty of rain keeps the Irish countryside green.

Like the United States, Ireland has four different seasons. All of its seasons are mild. The average summer temperature is 59° Fahrenheit (15° Celsius). In winter, the average temperature is 41° F (5° C). Compared with the coasts, inland areas are warmer in summer and colder in winter.

Irish People

About four million people live in the Republic of Ireland. Today, Ireland is a blend of the **cultures** of people who came from other parts of Europe over thousands of years.

A group of people called the Celts (seltz) came to Ireland more than two thousand years ago. Those people brought their laws, customs, and language to Ireland. Irish, spoken by many people in Ireland today, comes from the language of the Celts.

Ruins of old castles and forts are reminders of Ireland's past.

Road signs appear in both Irish and English, the two main languages of Ireland.

Did you know?

The feast day of Saint Patrick is a national holiday in Ireland. Saint Patrick is an important saint to the Roman Catholic people of the country.

People line the streets to watch the Saint Patrick's Day parade in Dublin.

Religion, family, and country are very important to the people of Ireland. Most people in the Republic of Ireland are Roman Catholic. Many of the rest belong to Protestant churches. Disagreements between Protestants and Catholics in Ireland and Northern Ireland caused fighting for many years.

School and Family

In the Republic of Ireland, children ages six to fifteen must attend school. The school day lasts six to seven hours. Children go to school Monday through Friday.

Primary school is for students up to age twelve. Children study math, reading, writing, computers, religion, and Irish history and culture. Classes are taught in English, but children also learn Irish. After school, some children play sports such as tennis and soccer. Others might take dance or music lessons.

Many children in Ireland go to schools run by the Catholic Church. The students at those schools usually wear uniforms.

Children enjoy playing sports after the school day is over. Rugby is a favorite.

After primary school, students attend secondary school. Many go on to college or have special job training.

Young people often live at home until they marry. Families eat meals and go to church together. They also gather to celebrate birthdays and holidays.

An average family in Ireland is made up of two parents and three or four children.

Families celebrate holidays, such as Saint Patrick's Day, together.

Did you know?

Ireland is home to about four million people. The country has more sheep than people!

Country Life

For hundreds of years, most Irish people lived and worked in the country. Today, fewer than half of the people in Ireland live on farms and in small villages.

Most farms in Ireland are small and family-owned. Potatoes, grain, sugar beets, and turnips are main crops. Some farmers also raise sheep, horses, and dairy and beef cattle.

In towns, people work in bakeries, shops, and **pubs**. Others work in their homes, knitting sweaters or making lace to sell to **tourists**.

Children help care for farm animals.

Some villagers knit fine lace or create other handmade goods. They sell those items to tourists.

Fishermen catch cod and other saltwater fish off Ireland's seacoast.

Pubs, markets, and shops line the streets of most villages. A church is usually at the center of town.

Near Ireland's coasts, lakes, and rivers, many people make their living by fishing. They catch trout, salmon, cod, and other types of fish.

Almost every Irish village has a church. Community life often centers around the church.

Did you know?

In the 1840s, a disease killed most of the Irish potato plants. Almost one million people starved to death in a **famine**. That time is called the Great Famine.

City Life

Today, more than half of the people in Ireland live in or near cities. Dublin is the capital. It is also the largest city in Ireland. Dublin is the center of government and culture. More than one million people live there.

Dublin has modern apartment houses and office buildings. It is also home to Ireland's oldest college. Dublin has many old churches and a castle from the 1200s.

Did you know?

One of the oldest books in the world is the Book of Kells. It is kept at Trinity College in Dublin.

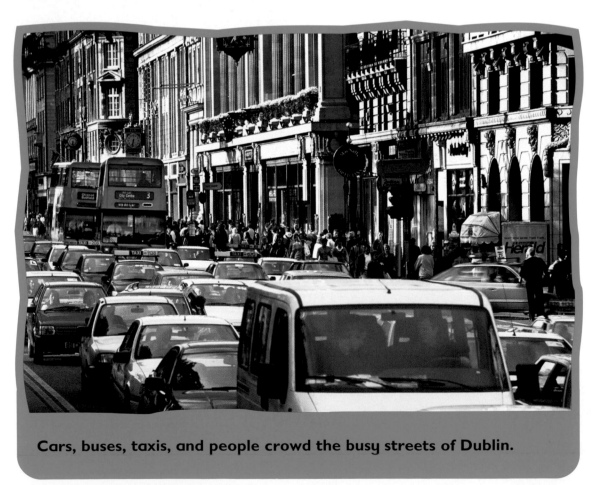

Cars, buses, taxis, and people crowd the busy streets of Dublin.

This bridge crosses the River Liffey in Dublin.

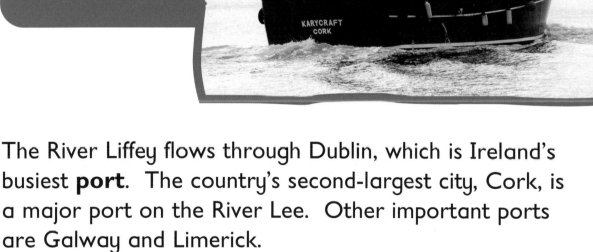

People travel on ferryboats to cross the Irish Sea.

The River Liffey flows through Dublin, which is Ireland's busiest **port**. The country's second-largest city, Cork, is a major port on the River Lee. Other important ports are Galway and Limerick.

In crowded cities, many people take buses or taxis to go to work. Airplanes fly to major airports in Dublin, Shannon, and Cork. People also travel by water. **Ferryboats** carry people across the Irish Sea to Great Britain.

Irish Houses

Most houses in Ireland are built of brick or cement. Those materials stand up well to rain, which falls often in Ireland. A typical house has four to seven rooms.

In Dublin, many people live in brick row houses. Those homes are built side by side. Other people live in tall apartment buildings or in large, modern houses outside the city.

In Dublin and other cities, many people live in row houses like these.

In the country, some people live in stone cottages with **thatched** roofs. Most modern country homes have **slate** or tile roofs. Large farmhouses are usually made of cement blocks or bricks.

Stone cottages dot the green countryside. Most have thatched roofs made of grass and straw.

Many homes are built of stone, brick, and cement. Those materials hold up well in Ireland's rainy weather.

Irish Food

Typically, Irish people eat big meals. Potatoes are often on the menu. Breakfast might include eggs, bacon, sausage, potatoes, and tomatoes. Sometimes the morning meal is a simple one of cereal and toast.

A common lunch is boiled salt pork, cabbage, and potatoes. Irish stew is a popular dish. It is made with lamb and vegetables. Turnips, breads, and dairy products are

People enjoy dining with friends at local restaurants.

Irish stew and brown bread make a tasty lunch.

Teatime is a daily custom in Ireland. Most people drink three to four cups of tea a day.

common foods, too. Many people enjoy drinking a cup of tea while eating cakes, tarts, and **scones**. Scones are biscuits that are served with butter or jam.

When Irish people eat out, they often enjoy fish-and-chips. That popular dish includes fried fish and French-fried potatoes. Many people gather in pubs, where they eat, drink, and visit with friends.

At Work

More than half of the people have jobs in health care, government, education, or tourism. They work in hospitals, schools, stores, banks, and restaurants.

Ireland is a world leader in computers and medicine. Factory workers make fine crystal glass, cement, linen, lace, and woolen goods.

World-famous crystal glass is made in the city of Waterford.

A worker puts together computers at a factory in Limerick.

A costumed guide tells tourists about Bunratty Castle and its past.

This farmer uses a wooden spade to dig peat.

Fishing, farming, and mining are other important businesses. Some people cut, dry, and sell peat. Peat is made from partly rotted plants. It is used for fuel and in gardens. Ireland **exports**, or sends to other countries, large amounts of certain metals.

Having Fun

Many people in Ireland enjoy watching and playing sports. **Gaelic** (GAY-lik) **football** is a very old sport that is still enjoyed today. It is a lot like soccer, but players can touch the ball. Another popular sport is **hurling**. Hurling is much like field hockey but faster. Soccer is a favorite team sport. Ireland's national soccer team has played in the World Cup games.

People in Ireland also like to watch horse racing. The Irish Derby is a famous race held in County Kildare.

Each year, crowds of people watch the Irish Derby horse race.

24

Irish step dancers wear colorful costumes and special shoes.

Visitors enjoy the gardens at Birr Castle. The castle has been a family home for more than five hundred years.

The Irish have fun listening and dancing to folk music. They also like going to concerts and plays. Favorite outdoor activities include hiking, biking, fishing, sailing, and horseback riding. Visiting Ireland's coasts and exploring its castles and forts are popular ways to spend a day.

Ireland: The Facts

• English and Irish are the two languages of Ireland. English is used most in everyday conversations.

• Ireland is a republic. Its president is the **head of state**. A prime minister handles the day-to-day running of the government.

• All of Ireland was once ruled by Great Britain. In 1921, Ireland was divided into two parts. Northern Ireland remained with Great Britain. (Great Britain and Northern Ireland are called the United Kingdom.) The southern part of Ireland became the Irish Free State. In 1949, it became the Republic of Ireland.

• People who are at least eighteen years old may vote in the nation's elections.

• The flag of the Republic of Ireland has three bars. They are green, white, and orange. The green bar stands for the Roman Catholic people. The orange bar stands for the Protestant people. The white bar is a symbol of the hope for peace between the two groups.

The flag of Ireland has bars of green, white, and orange.

• Ireland belongs to a group of countries called the European Union. Most of those countries, including Ireland, use the same currency, or money. It is called the **euro**. Euro paper money looks the same in those nations. The fronts of euro coins also look the same, but the backs of the coins are different. Each country has its own design. Irish euro coins have a picture of a harp, a symbol of Ireland's love for music.

The back of the Irish euro coin shows a harp. The harp is a symbol of Ireland.

The name *shamrock* comes from an Irish word that means "little clover."

Did you know?

The shamrock is a symbol of Ireland. This green plant with three leaves is said to bring good luck.

Glossary

counties – regions or districts in a state or country

cultures – the ways of living, beliefs, and arts of nations or groups of people

Emerald Isle – a nickname for Ireland that comes from the green color of the emerald jewel

euro – the currency, or money, used by many of the member nations of the European Union

exports – sells and sends goods to another country

famine – a great shortage of food

ferryboats – boats used to carry people, vehicles, or goods across water

Gaelic football – an ancient sport in Ireland that is a lot like soccer, except that players are allowed to handle the ball

head of state – the main representative of a country

hurling – an ancient sport in Ireland that is a lot like field hockey but faster

peat bogs – areas of wet, marshy land with partly rotted plant matter

port – a town or city where ships take on or unload goods

pubs – popular gathering places where people eat, drink, and talk with family and friends

republic – a kind of government in which decisions are made by the people of the country and their representatives

scones – quick breads that are usually cut into triangles

slate – a kind of rock that can easily be split into slabs for roofing

thatched – made of woven grass, straw, or reeds

tourists – people who travel to different places for fun

Find Out More

Enchanted Learning: Zoom School
www.zoomschool.com/europe/ireland

Information About Ireland
www.ireland-information.com/freegames.htm

KidsKonnect: Ireland Fast Facts
www.kidskonnect.com/Ireland/IrelandHome.html

Travel the World With A to Z Kids Stuff: Ireland
www.atozkidsstuff.com/ireland.html

Publisher's note to educators and parents: Our editors have carefully reviewed these Web sites to ensure that they are suitable for children. Many Web sites change frequently, however, and we cannot guarantee that a site's future contents will continue to meet our high standards of quality and educational value. Be advised that children should be closely supervised whenever they access the Internet.

My Map of Ireland

Photocopy or trace the map on page 31. Then write in the names of the countries, bodies of water, regions, cities, and land areas listed below. (Look at the map on page 5 if you need help.)

After you have written in the names of all the places, find some crayons and color the map!

Countries
Ireland
Northern Ireland
  (United Kingdom)

Bodies of Water
Atlantic Ocean
Irish Sea
River Lee
River Liffey
River Shannon

Counties
Clare
Kildare

Cities and Towns
Cork
Dublin
Galway
Limerick
Shannon
Waterford

Islands and Island Groups
Achill Island

Land Areas and Mountains
Carrantuohill
Cliffs of Moher

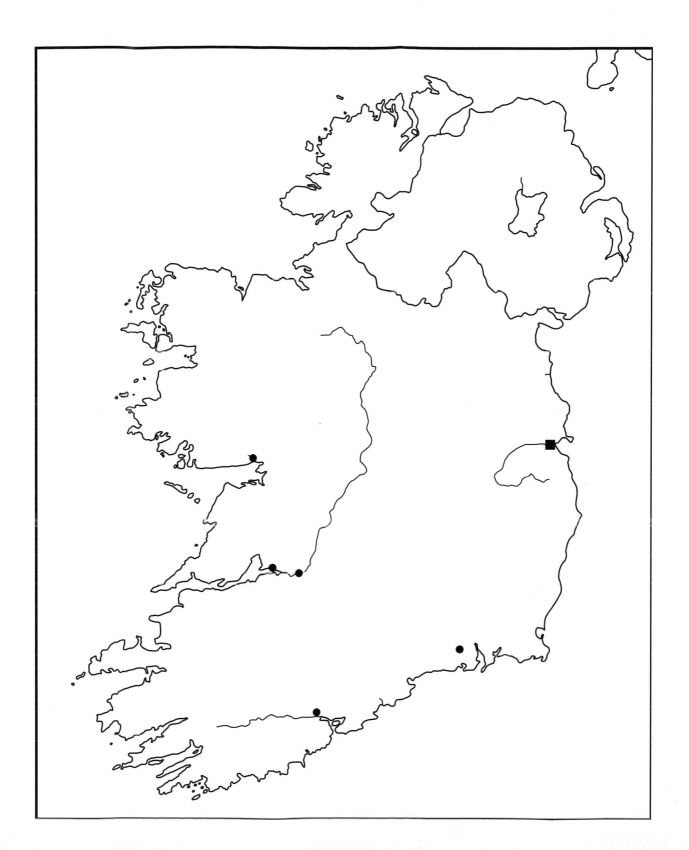

Index

airports 17

castles 10, 16,
   18, 23, 25
Celts 10
cities 4, 5, 16–17,
   18, 22
counties 5, 7, 24
countryside 6, 9,
   14–15, 19
currency 27

dance 25
Dublin 4, 5, 11,
   16–17, 18

factories 22
families 13
famine 15
farming 14–15,
   23
ferryboats 17
fishing 7, 15, 23
flag 26
food 20–21

government 4,
   5, 26
Great Britain 4, 5,
   17, 26

holidays 11, 13
houses 18–19

industries 22–23
Irish Sea 5, 17

lakes 7, 15
landscapes 6–7
languages 10–11,
   26
livestock 13, 14

mining 23
mountains 6

Northern Ireland
   4, 11, 26

peat 6, 23
population 10, 13
pubs 14, 15, 21

rain 7, 8–9, 19
religions 11, 12,
   13, 15
rivers 7, 15, 17

schools 12–13, 16
shamrock 27
sports 7, 12, 24–25

tourism 14, 22, 23
transportation
   16–17

United Kingdom
   4, 26

weather 8–9, 19
working 14, 15,
   22–23